WILD WEST

COLORING BOOK FOR ADULTS

Majestic **COLORING**

ISBN: 978-1519455383

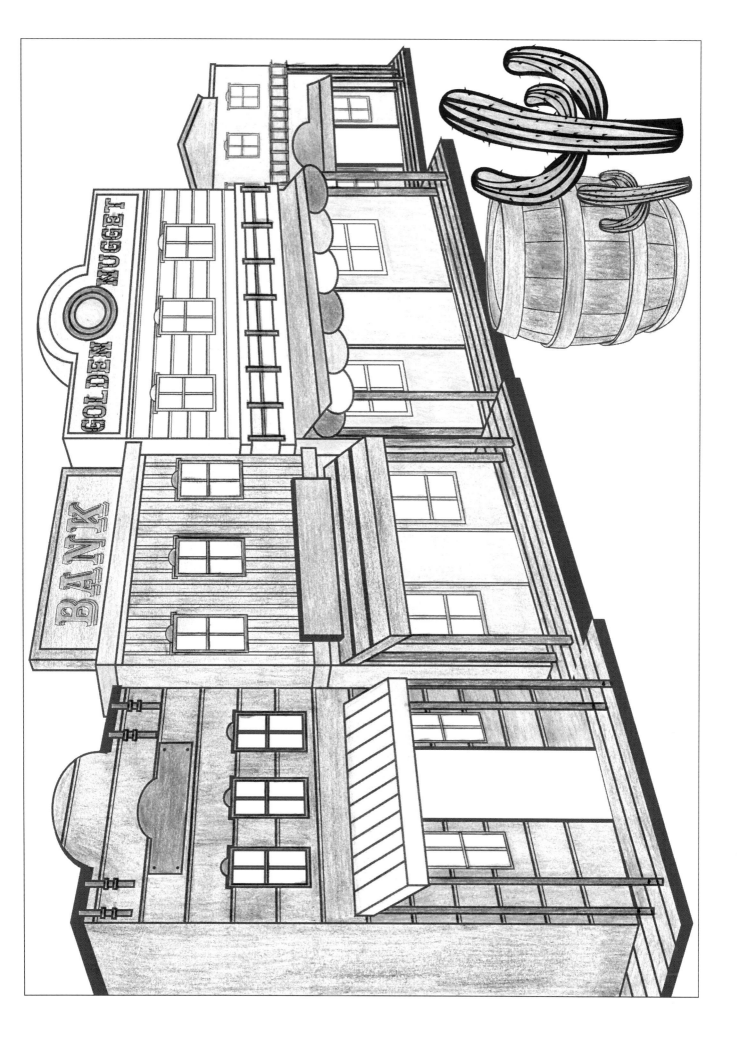

SHERIFF

LOREM COUNTY

DEPARTMENT

UNITED STATES OF AMERICA

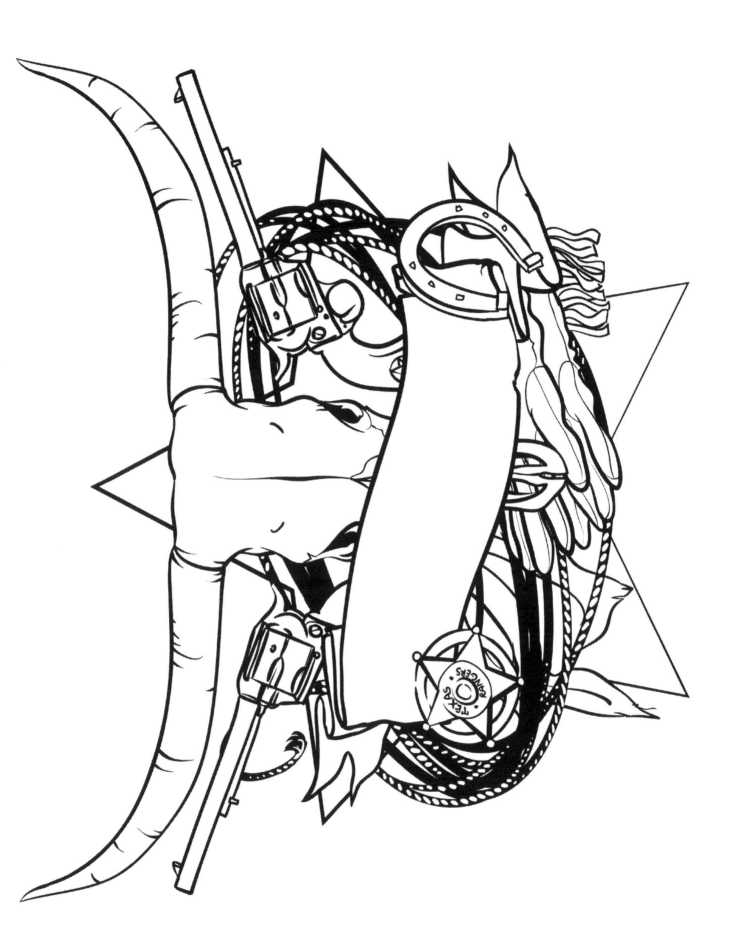

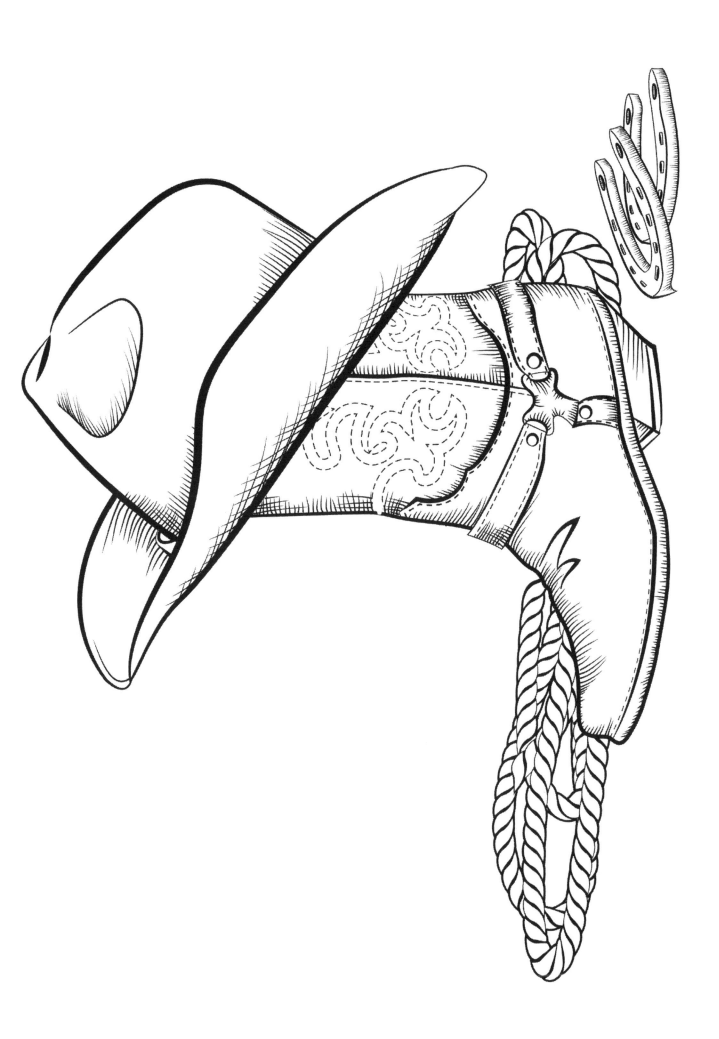

WANTED
DEAD OR ALIVE

ARMED AND VERY DANGEROUS

$10,000 CASH
REWARD

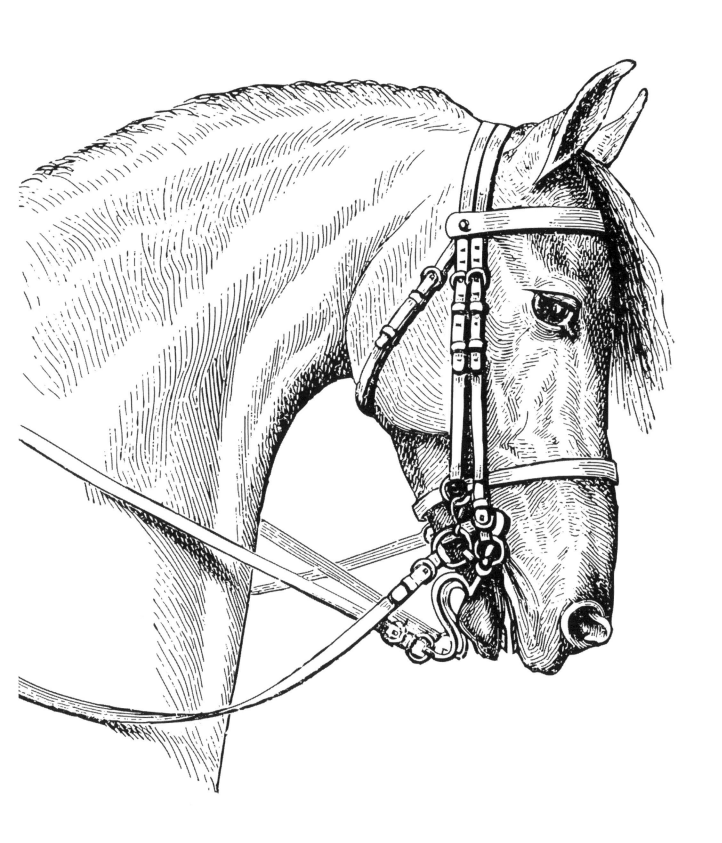

FREE DOWNLOAD

12 FUN DESIGNS FOR YOUR COLORING ENJOYMENT!

This 'n That Coloring Book for Grown-Ups is bundled up in one convenient PDF file to download and print at your leisure.

Sign up for our Majestic Coloring mailing list and get a free copy of **This 'n That Coloring Book for Grown-Ups**.

Click here to get started
http://majesticcoloring.com/thisnthat-free

Made in the USA
Monee, IL
27 September 2020